APOCALYPSE

CARLOS PELLAS

ISBN 978-1-0980-1321-9 (paperback)
ISBN 978-1-0980-1322-6 (digital)

Christian Faith Publishing, Inc.
832 Park Avenue
Meadville, PA 16335
www.christianfaithpublishing.com

Printed in the United States of America

CHAPTER 1

The book of Revelation by John, as translated by the American Standard Version, states: "The Revelation of Jesus Christ, which God gave him to show unto his servants, even the things which must shortly come to pass: and he sent and signified it by his angel unto his servant John; who bare witness of the word of God, and of the testimony of Jesus Christ, even of all things that he saw. Blessed is he that readeth, and they that hear the words of the prophecy, and keep the things that are written therein: for the time is at hand." *The Revelation* is defined as "an uncovering." *Servants* are defined as "slaves."

The book of Revelation by John, as translated by the American Standard Version, states: "John to the seven churches that are in Asia: Grace to you and peace, from him who is and who was and who is to come; and from the seven Spirits that are before his throne; and from Jesus Christ, who is the faithful witness, the firstborn of the dead, and the ruler of the kings of the earth. Unto him that loveth us, and loosed us from our sins by his blood; and he made us to be a kingdom, to be priests unto his God and Father; to him be the glory and the dominion for ever and ever. Amen. Behold, he cometh with the clouds; and every eye shall see him, and they that pierced him; and all the tribes of the earth shall mourn over him." *Churches* are defined as "assemblies, (religious) congregations." *Amen* is defined as "truly."

The book of Revelation by John, as translated by the American Standard Version, states: "And having turned I saw seven golden candlesticks; and in the midst of the candlesticks one like unto a son of man, clothed with a garment down to the foot, and girt about at the breasts with a golden girdle. And his head and his hair were white as white wool, white as snow; and his eyes were as a flame of fire; and his feet like unto burnished brass, as if it had been refined in a furnace; and his voice as the voice of many waters. And he had in his right hand seven stars: and out of his mouth proceeded a sharp two-edged sword: and his countenance was as the sun shineth in his strength." *Girdle* is defined as "belt."

The book of Revelation by John, as translated by the American Standard Version, states: "And I saw in the right hand of him that sat on the throne a book written within and on the back, sealed with seven seals. And I saw a strong angel proclaiming with a great voice, Who is worthy to open the book, and to loose the seals thereof? And no one in the heaven, or on the earth, or under the earth, was able to open the book, or to look thereon. And I wept much, because no one was found worthy to open the book, or to look thereon: and one of the elders saith unto me, Weep not; behold, the Lion that is of the tribe of Judah, the Root of David, hath overcome to open the book and the seven seals thereof." The book of Revelation by John, as translated by the American Standard Version, states: "And when he opened the seventh seal, there followed a silence in heaven about the space of half an hour. And I saw the seven angels that stand before God; and there were given unto them seven trumpets." The book of Revelation by John, as translated by the American Standard Version, states: "And I saw another strong angel coming down out of heaven, arrayed with a cloud; and the rainbow was upon his head, and his face was as the sun, and his feet as pillars of fire; and he had in his hand a little book open: and he set his right foot upon the sea, and his left upon the earth; and he cried with a great voice, as a lion roareth: and when he cried, the seven thunders uttered their voices. And when the seven thunders uttered their voices, I was about to write: and I heard a voice from heaven saying, Seal up the things which the seven thunders uttered, and write them not. And the angel that I saw standing upon the sea and upon the earth lifted up his right hand to heaven, and sware by him that liveth for ever and ever, who created the heaven and the things that are therein, and the earth and the things that are therein, and the sea and the things that are therein, that there shall be delay no longer: but in the days of the voice of the seventh angel, when he is about to sound, then is finished the mystery of God, according to the good tidings which he declared to his servants the prophets." Jesus is the Root and the Offspring of David.

The book of Revelation by John, as translated by the American Standard Version, states: "And a great sign was seen in heaven: a woman arrayed with the sun, and the moon under her feet, and upon her head a crown of twelve stars; and she was with child; and she crieth out, travailing in birth, and in pain to be delivered." On September 23, 2017, the constellation Virgo, the sun, the moon, the constellation Leo, the planet Mercury, the planet Venus, the planet Mars and the planet Jupiter aligned to fulfill this prophecy.

The book of Revelation by John, as translated by the American Standard Version, states: "And there was seen another sign in heaven: and behold, a great red dragon, having seven heads and ten horns, and upon his heads seven diadems. And his tail draweth the third part of the stars of heaven, and did cast them to the earth: and the dragon standeth before the woman that is about to be delivered, that when she is delivered he may devour her child." Deneb, from the Arabic word dhanab, a tail, is a star in the constellation Cygnus.

The book of Revelation by John, as translated by the American Standard Version, states: "And she was delivered of a son, a man child, who is to rule all the nations with a rod of iron: and her child was caught up unto God, and unto his throne." *Was caught up* is defined as "to seize, snatch away."

The book of Revelation by John, as translated by the American Standard Version, states: "And there was war in heaven: Michael and his angels going forth to war with the dragon; and the dragon warred and his angels; And they prevailed not, neither was their place found anymore in heaven. And the great dragon was cast down, the old serpent, he that is called the Devil and Satan, the deceiver of the whole world; he was cast down to the earth, and his angels were cast down with him." *Devil* is defined as "slanderous, accusing falsely."

CHAPTER 2

The book of Revelation by John, as translated by the American Standard Version, states: "And the dragon waxed wroth with the woman, and went away to make war with the rest of her seed, that keep the commandments of God, and hold the testimony of Jesus: and he stood upon the sand of the sea. And I saw a beast coming up out of the sea, having ten horns, and seven heads, and on his horns ten diadems, and upon his heads names of blasphemy. And the beast which I saw was like unto a leopard, and his feet were as the feet of a bear, and his mouth as the mouth of a lion: and the dragon gave him his power, and his throne, and great authority." *Beast* is defined as "wild beast."

The book of Daniel, as translated by the American Standard Version, states: "I considered the horns, and, behold, there came up among them another horn, a little one, before which three of the first horns were plucked up by the roots: and, behold, in this horn were eyes like the eyes of a man, and a mouth speaking great things." *Daniel* is defined as "God is my judge."

The book of Revelation by John, as translated by the American Standard Version, states: "Here is wisdom. He that hath understanding, let him count the number of the beast; for it is the number of a man: and his number is Six hundred and sixty and six." 666 is the number of the man of lawlessness.

CHAPTER 3

The first epistle of John, as translated by the American Standard Version, states: "Little children, it is the last hour: and as ye heard that antichrist cometh, even now have there arisen many antichrists; whereby we know that it is the last hour. They went out from us, but they were not of us; for if they had been of us, they would have continued with us: but they went out, that they might be made manifest that they all are not of us. And ye have an anointing from the Holy One, and ye know all the things. I have not written unto you because ye know not the truth, but because ye know it, and because no lie is of the truth. Who is the liar but he that denieth that Jesus is the Christ? This is the antichrist, even he that denieth the Father and the Son. Whosoever denieth the Son, the same hath not the Father: he that confesseth the Son hath the Father also." The antichrist is equated to the man of lawlessness.

The first epistle to the Thessalonians by Paul, as translated by the American Standard Version, states: "For the Lord himself shall descend from heaven, with a shout, with the voice of the archangel, and with the trump of God: and the dead in Christ shall rise first; then we that are alive, that are left, shall together with them be caught up in the clouds, to meet the Lord in the air: and so shall we ever be with the Lord." *Shout* is defined as "shout of command."

The second epistle to the Thessalonians by Paul, as translated by the Holman Christian Standard Bible, states: "Therefore, we ourselves boast about you among God's churches—about your endurance and faith in all the persecutions and afflictions you endure. It is a clear evidence of God's righteous judgment that you will be counted worthy of God's kingdom, for which you also are suffering, since it is righteous for God to repay with affliction those who afflict you and to reward with rest you who are afflicted, along with us. This will take place at the revelation of the Lord Jesus from heaven with His powerful angels, taking vengeance with flaming fire on those who don't know God and on those who don't obey the gospel of our Lord Jesus. These will pay the penalty of eternal destruction from the Lord's presence and from His glorious strength in that day when He comes to be glorified by His saints and to be admired by all those who have believed, because our testimony among you was believed." *Gospel* is defined as "good news."

The second epistle to the Thessalonians by Paul, as translated by the Holman Christian Standard Bible, states: "Now concerning the coming of our Lord Jesus Christ and our being gathered to Him: We ask you, brothers, not to be easily upset in mind or troubled, either by a spirit or by a message or by a letter as if from us, alleging that the Day of the Lord has come. Don't let anyone deceive you in any way. For that day will not come unless the apostasy comes first and the man of lawlessness is revealed, the son of destruction. He opposes and exalts himself above every so-called god or object of worship, so that he sits in God's sanctuary, publicizing that he himself is God. Don't you remember that when I was still with you I told you about this? And you know what currently restrains him, so that he will be revealed in his time. For the mystery of lawlessness is already at work, but the one now restraining will do so until he is out of the way, and then the lawless one will be revealed. The Lord Jesus will destroy him with the breath of His mouth and will bring him to nothing with the brightness of His coming. The coming of the lawless one is based on Satan's working, with all kinds of false miracles, signs, and wonders, and with every unrighteous deception among those who are perishing." *Apostasy* is defined as "defection, revolt."

CHAPTER 4

The book of Revelation by John, as translated by the American Standard Version, states: "And I saw another angel flying in mid heaven, having eternal good tidings to proclaim unto them that dwell on the earth, and unto every nation and tribe and tongue and people; and he saith with a great voice, Fear God, and give him glory; for the hour of his judgement is come: and worship him that made the heaven and the earth and sea and fountains of waters. And another, a second angel, followed, saying, Fallen, fallen is Babylon the Great, that hath made all the nations to drink of the wine of the wrath of her fornication." *Wrath* is defined as "passion."

The book of Revelation by John, as translated by the American Standard Version, states: "And I heard a great voice out of the temple, saying to the seven angels, Go ye, and pour out the seven bowls of the wrath of God into the earth. And the first went, and poured out his bowl into the earth; and it became a noisome and grievous sore upon the men that had the mark of the beast, and that worshipped his image. And the second poured out his bowl into the sea; and it became blood as of a dead man; and every living soul died, even the things that were in the sea. And the third poured out his bowl into the rivers and the fountains of the waters; and it became blood. And I heard the angel of the waters saying, Righteous art thou, who art and who wast, thou Holy One, because thou didst thus judge: for they poured out the blood of the saints and the prophets, and blood hast thou given them to drink: they are worthy. And I heard the altar saying, Yea, O Lord God, the Almighty, true and righteous are thy judgements. And the fourth poured out his bowl upon the sun; and it was given unto him to scorch men with fire. And men were scorched with great heat: and they blasphemed the name of God who hath the power over these plagues; and they repented not to give him glory. And the fifth poured out his bowl upon the throne of the beast; and his kingdom was darkened; and they gnawed their tongues for pain, and they blasphemed the God of heaven because of their pains and their sores; and they repented not of their works. And the sixth poured out his bowl upon the great river, the river Euphrates; and the water thereof was dried up, that the way might be made ready for the kings that come from the sunrising. And I saw coming out of the mouth of the dragon, and out of the mouth of the beast, and out of the mouth of the false prophet, three unclean spirits, as it were frogs: for they are spirits of demons, working signs; which go forth unto the kings of the whole world, to gather them together unto the war of the great day of God, the Almighty. (Behold, I come as a thief. Blessed is he that watcheth, and keepeth his garments, lest he walk naked, and they see his shame.) And they gathered them together into the place which is called in Hebrew Har-magedon. And the seventh poured out his bowl upon the air; and there came forth a great voice out of the temple, from the throne, saying, It is done: and there were lightnings, and voices, and thunders; and there was a great earthquake, such as was not since there were men upon the earth, so great an earthquake, so mighty. And the great city was divided into three parts, and the cities of the nations fell: and Babylon the Great was remembered in the sight of God, to give unto her the cup of the wine of the fierceness of his wrath." The book of Revelation by John, as translated by the American Standard Version, states: "And there came one of the seven angels that had the seven bowls, and he spake with me, saying, Come hither, I will show thee the judgement of the great harlot that sitteth upon many waters; with whom the kings of the earth committed fornication, and they that dwell in the earth were made drunken with the wine of her fornication. And he carried me away in the Spirit into a wilderness: and I saw a woman sitting upon a scarlet-colored beast, full of names of blasphemy, having seven heads and ten horns. And the woman was arrayed in purple and scarlet, and decked with gold and precious stone and pearls, having in her hand a golden cup full of abominations, even the unclean things of her fornication, and upon her forehead a name written, Mystery, Babylon the Great, the

Mother of the Harlots and of the Abominations of the Earth. And I saw the woman drunken with the blood of the saints, and with the blood of the martyrs of Jesus." The clergy of the Roman Catholic Church is dressed in purple and scarlet.

ABOUT THE AUTHOR

CARLOS FRANCISCO PELLAS was born on June 8, 1979, in Miami, Florida, United States of America. He is the author of one faith-based work.

CPSIA information can be obtained
at www.ICGtesting.com
Printed in the USA
LVHW012059080222
710535LV00001B/120

9 781098 013219